Python Data Analysis

An Introduction to Computer Science: Learn Step By Step How to Use Python Programming Language, Pandas, and How You Can Use Them For Machine Learning

Steve Eddison

Table of Contents

Conclusion

Introduction

Congratulations on purchasing *Python Data Analysis* and thank you for doing so.

The following chapters will discuss everything that you need to know about working with data analysis and how this can help to change up your business. You may have spent some time collecting data and storing it for a while now. But just having that data sit there, without seeing what insights and information are hidden inside is not going to do you any good at all. When you are able to finally get to that data, and complete your own data analysis, that is when the true magic will begin. And the Python coding language will be just the tool that you need to create strong algorithms and models to sort through the data and find those hidden patterns.

Working with data analysis can be an in-depth process, and sometimes it is a bit scary to think about the kind of work and dedication that needs to happen. But when you are able to learn some of the basics that come with that data analysis, and you implement in the Python language to help you create strong, efficient, and fast models, you can complete your data analysis in no time, and use those predictions and insights for your advantage.

In this guidebook, we are going to take some time to explore what data analysis is all about. We will start out with a little introduction to the Python coding language, and some of the benefits that we are able to see when we choose this language over another option to help us to work on the data analysis. We can then move on to looking at some of the steps that you need to take in order to install Python on your own computer with ease. We can also look at a discussion on the benefits and the disadvantages of using Python on our data analysis, and you will quickly see that the benefits far outweigh any reason not to work with Python on this process.

From there, we are going to move into some of the basics that come with data analysis. We will explore what this data analysis is all about, how we can work with it, some of the steps that come in data analysis, and some of the reasons that a company would choose to implement this kind of analysis in their own business to see some results.

Some other topics that are explored in this guidebook to help you get a good start on your data analysis includes an introduction to the Pandas library, and a look at how you are able to install this library on your own computer, the basics of working with Python on a database and extracting some of the information that you would like out of that source, how to work with machine learning, and the importance of a predictive analysis in getting all of the work done. All of these topics can come together and will utilize some of the features of Python, to help you get through one of the most efficient and successful data analysis that you need.

Working with Python data analytics can be a great way to help your business get ahead and for you to get some of the results that you are looking for in the process. When you are ready to get started with this data analysis and to see how the Python language is able to help you out with all of this, make sure to check out this guidebook to get started.

There are plenty of books on this subject on the market, thanks again for choosing this one! Every effort was made to ensure it is full of as much useful information as possible, please enjoy it!

Chapter 1: What Is the Python Language

When it comes to working with your data analysis, it is important to have a good coding language that you are able to handle, one that is able to take on all of the complexities of your analysis, before you even get started. This is going to ensure that you are able to read through the data and see what information is there for you to utilize and benefit from and how to create the model that will get all of this work done.

There are a number of different coding languages that you are able to work with to get this done. But one of the best to help you reach your goals is going to be the Python coding language. This is a simple language that has been designed with the beginner in mind and is meant to help you not only learn how to code quickly, while still handling some of the complexities that are going to be present when we first learn how to work with data analysis. With this in mind, let's take a look at the Python coding language and how we are able to use this to help us benefit from data analysis.

What is the Python Language?

If you have done any research into the world of programming, it is likely that you have seen a lot of different types of programming languages and that all of them are thought to be some of the best in the industry. So, what is going to make it so that Python is ahead of the game, and the one that we want to pick above the others for working on data analysis? This section is going to spend some time looking at Python and how it can set itself apart from some of the other coding languages that you may try to use.

The Python coding language is freely available, meaning that you are able to download it onto your computer without having to worry about any extra costs. It is also going to be a great method to solve all of the problems you have, or any projects, with your computer and ensures that doing so is as easy and painless as writing out the thoughts you have about that solution. You are able to write out the code once and have it available to run on almost any computer you would like, without needing to make big changes to the code that you are working on.

Python is considered a general-purpose programming language that is set up to work on any modern computer operating system. It is usable for a lot of different things like processing the text that you want, handling images and numbers, dealing with scientific data, and pretty much anything else that you would like to save on your computer.

Just because working with this language is simple to do doesn't mean that you should ignore it and not see the value that comes with this kind of language. It is actually used in some of the daily operations of the Google Search Engine we all know and love, with many of the videos that we see on YouTube, the New York Stock Exchange, and even some of the programs that NASA is going to use this language.

Python is also considered an interpreted language. This means that it is not going to be converted over to a code that is readable by your computer before the program is run, but this happens when we reach runtime. In the past, this type of language would be known as a scripting language, imitating its use was for some of the smaller and trivial tasks that you didn't need a powerful code to get it done.

However, you will find that this has changed in modern times and there are a lot of powerful things that you are able to work with Python on. Programming languages such as Python have been able to force a big change in the nomenclature that comes with these kinds of languages. Increasingly, there are a lot of large applications that are now being written out almost exclusively with this language. Some of the different ways that we are able to apply the use of the Python language in our daily lives is going to include:

1. Programming the CGI for web applications.
2. Building up our own RSS Reader
3. Working with any of the files that we have in Python

4. Creating a calendar that needs to be in HTML.
5. Reading from and then writing to the database that is known as PostgreSQL
6. Reading and writing to the database of MySQL

There may be a lot of other coding languages that we are able to work with overtime, but when it comes to handling data science and some of the analysis that we are going to do with all of this data, you will find that Python is going to be one of the best languages to focus on. When you are ready to work on your own data analysis and help your business to thrive.

The Benefits of the Python Language

The next thing that we need to take a quick look at while we are here is some of the benefits that come with using the Python coding language. There may be a lot of different programming and coding languages that we can use, and many of them are able to handle specialized tasks in coding that can make life easier. But Python is one of the best to use, especially when it comes to things like data science. We will take a closer look at some of the benefits that come with the Python coding language when handling a data analysis later on, but for now, we are going to look at some of the benefits of doing any kind of coding with Python.

There are a number of benefits that you will get when it is time to choose the Python language as your choice for coding. It is one of the most popular coding languages out there and will make it easier to handle pretty much any programming that you would like, whether you are working with data analysis, data science, machine learning, artificial intelligence, deep learning, or another topic along the way. Some of the benefits that you can enjoy when working with the Python coding language include:

1. It is easy to learn. If you have never spent any time working with coding in the past, but you would like to learn how to do some programming to work on data science, then the Python language is one of the best options for you to choose from. It is going to ensure that you are able to handle all of the parts of data analysis, in a format that is easy for even a beginner to get started on.

2. There is a lot of power behind the language: Even though we just spent some time talking about how easy this language is to learn, this shouldn't scare you away from using this language to help out with some of your machine learning and data analysis kinds of tasks. This language definitely has the power that you are looking for to handle these tasks and more. You may be surprised at the kind of coding that you are able to do with Python after looking at a few codes and seeing how simple they are to learn.

3. There is a large community of developers to help: Because of the popularity that comes with the Python language, there is already a large community of programmers and developers,

with varying degrees of experience in Python, available to help. If you get stuck on a coding problem, need help troubleshooting the work that you are doing, have a question, or want to learn how to do something new with this language, then there will always be someone there to help out. This makes it easier for a beginner to get started in this language as well.

4. It can work with a variety of libraries: The standard library that comes with Python is a great option to work with and can handle many of the codes and programming that you want to do. In addition, when it is time to handle tasks like machine learning and data analysis, you will find that there are plenty of libraries and extensions that can handle these tasks while still using the Python language. This ensures that you gain all of the capabilities that are needed to handle this language and make it easier to get the work done that you would like.

5. It can connect with other coding languages when needed. While Python has a lot of strength to handle the tasks that you would like on its own, there are going to be times, especially with a few of the data science libraries, where you

will need to combine it with other coding languages. Python can do this without any problems at all, making it easier to handle some of the more complex tasks that you want to do while handling a data analysis.

There is a lot of potentials that are going to come up when we work with Python. You will be able to work with it to handle most of the projects that you would like to work with when it is time to handle some data science work as well. Data science and Python are able to go hand in hand together and will be able to bring your business into the future. But we need to take our time to see some of the benefits of working with Python, and how you are able to combine these two topics together.

As we can see, there are a lot of benefits that come with the Python coding language, and we have just started with some of the best ones! Working with Python is a great option to handle a lot of the coding needs that you want to take care of and will ensure that you will be able to get all of your coding needs done in no time at all. When you are ready to work with data analysis, and even some of the basics of coding, then the Python coding language is going to be one of the best options for you.

Chapter 2: How to Install Python and Get Started with Coding

Now that we have had a bit of time to take a look at the Python coding language, how it works, and some of the benefits of choosing this language over one of the other options that you have, it is time to explore more about how to get the Python language installed on your computer. Going through the process may take a bit of time, but you will quickly find that it is painless and easy to do. As an added bonus, Python is able to work on any operating system that you would like to work with, which means that you can easily download it to any system that you would like, without having to worry about compatibility issues or anything else like that.

With this in mind, it is time for us to take a look at the steps that we can take in order to install our Python code and get it ready to work on any operating system that we would like to use.

Installing On a Linux Operating System

We can also work with the Linux operating system. This may not be an operating system that is as good as the other two options, but it is going to be a great one when it is time to work with the Python language and some of the neat things that you are able to do with it. Many of those who do use the Linux system is going to use it in conjunction with one of the other options on their computer. No matter how you decide to use it though, you will find that it is a great option to help you do some of the codings in Python for your data analysis.

If you do plan on using the Linux operating system to help you download and install everything that you need to do some coding in Python, you will find that working with the installation is going to be pretty easy. We have to just work with a few lines of code and then check on a few things to ensure that the system is set and ready to go, and then you will be able to complete any of the programs and coding that you would like.

With all of this in mind, the first step that we are going to take here is to check out the operating system and see whether we have a Python 3 version on it or not. To check for this, we are going to keep it simple with one line of code. The command that will help us to check out whether we already have a version of Python 3 available on our system or not includes the following:

```
$ python3 - - version
```

If you are on Ubuntu 16.10 or newer, then it is a simple process to install Python 3.6. you just need to use the following commands:

```
$ sudo apt-get update
$ sudo apt-get install Python3.6
```

If you are relying on an older version of Ubuntu or another version, then you may want to work with the deadsnakes PPA, or another tool, to help you download the Python 3.6 version. The code that you need to do this includes:

```
$ sudo apt-get install software-properties-common
```

```
$ sudo add-apt repository ppa:deadsnakes/ppa
# sudo apt-get update
$ sudo apt-get install python3.6
```

The thing that we need to consider here is that if you are working with any of the other distributions that are available with Linux, whether it is now or at an earlier time, then it is likely that you will find that the Python 3 is already on your system and it is ready for you to utilize. Knowing this is going to save you a lot of time and can make things easier. If not, you are able to use some of the codes that we have above to get this put on your Linux system and ready to use for your own needs.

Installing On a Mac Operating System

The second system that we are going to take a look at when it is time to set up Python is the Mac OS X. If you are working with an Apple computer and you would like to be able to utilize the Python language and get it to work the best for you, then these are the steps that we need to go through. If your system is a bit newer, then you may find that there is going to be a version of Python that is set up and ready to go on your computer. This is usually some version of Python 2, but you will have to go through and double-check which one was added to your system at the time it was developed. In order to check out which Python version is on your Mac operating system; you will just need to use the following code below:

python – V

Putting this into your command terminal will help you to see the number of the version that you are working with. You can choose to just work with that environment if you would like, or you can go through and install Python 3 on your system. To check if there is already a Python 3 version on your computer, just type in the following prompt to your terminal when it comes up:

Python3 – V

When you do this coding, you will find that the default is not going to be a version of Python 3 on your computer, but rather a version of Python 2. This doesn't mean that you are out of luck and can't work with Python 3, it just means that we need to go through a couple of steps in order to get this Python 3 installed on your system and ready to go. If you are ready to install your Python 3 on the system, the first step is to visit www.python.org and look for your operating system and the version of Python 3 that you would like to work with.

Now, there are going to be a few different websites that you can choose to go to when you would like to install Python and get it to work for your needs. However, the website above is going to ensure that you get Python and all of the necessary files that you need to get started. and they are all for free. You can go with another option if you would like, but you need to double-check whether they are going to allow you to work with all of the files that you need, like the compiler and the IDLE, and whether it is going to cost you any money to use these or not.

Being able to run the shell and the IDLE, and all of the other files that you want with Python, on your operating system is going to be dependent on what version of this language you would like to go with. And you do have the option of working with some of the other changes based on what your own personal preferences are all about. You are able to use some of the following commands to help us make sure that the applications for our shell and our IDLE are ready to go:

- For Python 2.X just type in "Idle"
- For Python 3.X, just type in "idle3"

As we mentioned before, when you download and install Python 3, you are going to install IDLE as a standard application in the Applications folder. In order to start this program from your desktop, you simply need to open up that folder and then double click on the IDLE application.

Installing On a Windows Operating System

The final operating system that we are going to explore here is how we are able to work with the Windows programs along with Python. Since there are many individuals who are going to work with the Windows system on their personal computers, it is good to know that they have the option to download and use Python as they need.

One thing to remember here though is that Python is not going to come automatically on your system as it did with the other operating systems. This is because Windows has its own coding language that they install on their system. This doesn't mean that Python is not going to work on Windows, it just means that you will have to go through the proper steps to get it downloaded, and won't get lucky with it already being on your system.

The steps for working with the Windows Operating System may seem a bit complex, but this doesn't mean that it is too hard for you to work with at all. It simply means that you need to take a few minutes, maybe five to ten, in order to get the Python program up and running and ready to handle. This isn't that big of a deal though and you will find that when it is all said and done, Python will work great on your system without any issues. With this in mind, some of the steps that you need to use in order to work with the Python language and your Windows operating system includes:

1. To set this up, you need to visit the official Python download page and grab the Windows

installer. You can choose to do the latest version of Python 3, or go with another option. By default, the installer is going to provide you with the 32-bit version of Python, but you can choose to switch this to the 64-bit version if you wish. The 32-bit is often best to make sure that there aren't any compatibility issues with the older packages, but you can experiment if you wish.

2. Now right-click on the installer and select "Run as Administrator". There are going to be two options to choose from. You will want to pick out "Customize Installation"

3. On the following screen, make sure all of the boxes under "Optional Features" are clicked and then click to move on.

4. While under Advanced Options" you should pick out the location where you want Python to be installed. Click on Install. Give it some time to finish and then close the installer.

5. Next, set the PATH variable for the system so that it includes directories that will include packages and other components that you will need later. To do this use the following instructions:

a. Open up the Control Panel. Do this by clicking on the taskbar and typing in Control Panel. Click on the icon.

b. Inside the Control Panel, search for Environment. Then click on Edit the System Environment Variables. From here, you can click on the button for Environment Variables.

c. Go to the section for User Variables. You can either edit the PATH variable that is there, or you can create one.

d. If there isn't a variable for PATH on the system, then create one by clicking on New. Make the name for the PATH variable and add it to the directories that you want. Click on close all the control Panel dialogs and move on.

6. Now you can open up your command prompt. Do this by clicking on Start Menu, then Windows System, and then Command Prompt. Type in "python". This is going to load up the Python interpreter for you.

These may sound like a lot of steps to get things done, but it doesn't take that long and it will ensure that you are able to get the Python coding language set up and ready to go on your Windows computer.

As you can see, adding the Python coding to any operating system, whether we are talking about the Mac operating system, Linux, or Windows. All of these are important operating systems that we are able to work with, and they are going to be able to help us get things done. And the fact that we are able to use any of them in order to work with the Python coding language and help with our data science project makes them even better in the end.

Chapter 3: What is Data Analysis?

Now that we have been able to take some time to look at the Python coding language and all that comes with it, it is time for us to move on to some of the basics of data analysis. Many companies are jumping on board with using this kind of analysis to get themselves ahead and to make it easier to get results that actually help their business. Instead of just collecting the data and hoping for the best, the data analysis can help us take that information, and sort through it in a manner that helps us understand what is inside.

Often when a business is dealing with big data, it is going to be so vast and so varied that it is hard to imagine going through that information and figuring out what is inside at all. And imagining doing this manually, without having any algorithms or models to help you out is pretty much impossible. But with the process of data science, we are better able to go through the information, no matter how much information there is, and learn the best way to handle the data, the best-hidden patterns, and insights, and make more informed decisions for our business overall.

To keep it simple, data analysis is going to be the practice where a company can take their raw data and then order and organize it. When the data is organized in this manner, and run through a predictive model, it is going to help the company extract useful information out of it. The process of organizing and thinking about our data is going to be very important as it is the key to helping us understand what the data does and does not contain at any given time.

Many companies have been collecting data for a long time. They may gather this data from their customers, from surveys, from social media, and many other locations. And while collecting the data is an important step that we need to focus on as well, another thing to consider is what we can do with the data. You can collect all of the data that you would like, but if it just sits in your cloud or a data warehouse and is never mined or used, then it is going to become worthless to you, and you wasted a lot of time and money trying to figure it all out.

This is where data analysis will come in. it is able to take all of that raw data and actually, put it to some good use. It will use various models and algorithms, usually with the help of machine learning and Python, in order to help us to understand what important insights and information are found in our data, and how we are able to utilize these for our own benefit.

There are a lot of different methods and approaches that we are able to use when it comes to data analysis, and many of them can be legitimate ways to handle any of the data that we are dealing with. With this in mind though, we need to be careful with the data that we are using and how we try to manipulate it or not. It is actually pretty easy to go through the analysis phase and try to manipulate the data, and sometimes it is hard to figure out whether you are doing this or not. But if you are not careful about keeping the manipulation out of your work and out of the data analysis that you are doing, it can skew the results, and you will make poor decisions for your whole business.

Because of this reason, and many others, it is always important that when you are working on your data analysis that you are careful not to have any prejudices or notions about what should happen ahead of time. And if you have a data scientist on your team who does the data analysis for you, it is important to really pay attention to the way that they are presenting the information and to think through the information about the data as critically as possible. You want to make sure that all of the conclusions that are drawn are accurate, reliable and will actually help you to make some good business decisions along the way.

Another thing that we need to consider here is the raw data that we are using. Raw data is going to take on a variety of forms. This could include posts from social media, responses to the surveys that you send out, your observations, and even measurements. This is all a good thing because it allows you to gather your information from a wide variety of sources in the process.

When we have the data in its raw form, we should know that this information is going to be really useful to our whole business. But it is also going to be overwhelming at times. Over the course of our process with data analysis, the raw data is going to be taken from its original form and ordered in a way that is the most useful. Leaving it in the raw format, especially if you gathered the data from more than one location, is going to cause some problems and the algorithm that you choose is not going to work that well at all.

So, for example, we may find that if we sent out a survey that we asked customers to fill out, we would want to tally up the votes and see where people made their choices. This allows those who are making the big decisions to see, hopefully at a glance if you added in the visuals, how many people answered the survey in the first place, and how those people responded to the different questions that were asked.

During the process of working to organize your data, it is likely that you will start to see some big trends start to emerge. These are important to focus on because they will allow you to figure out what decisions you should make in the future when it comes to your business, and how you will help provide the best products and services for your customers. These trends are then going to be highlighted in any writeups that happen with the data so that those who need to use the information and are reading about the results of the data analysis can take note.

We can take a look at an example of how this is going to work. When we look at a causal survey about ice cream and what preferences men and women have with this, you may find that more women, compared to men, had a fondness for eating strawberry ice cream. Depending on what you are doing this whole process for and what results you are hoping to get, it could end up being a major point of interest for the researcher.

Once we know this kind of relationship is in place, we are then able to work with the process of modeling the data. This can be done with a variety of tools, including mathematics, and if you use them in the right way, it is possible that these are going to exaggerate the points of interest so that we can see them a bit easier as we go through this process.

Once we have had some time to go through all of this information and highlight some of the big trends that are found in our data, it is time to work with how it is going to be presented. Of course, we will want to do some kind of textual writeup of the information. This ensures that the people using it to make big decisions are able to see the information and understand what is there. This text needs to include information on the process you took, the resources that you used, and more. This is an important part to add to the process because it ensures that we are going to be able to get the best results and will help whoever is looking at the information to have some background to research as well.

You will also need to use some visuals to help out with this process as well. Things like charts and graphs make it easier to see some of the more complex types of relationships that are going to show up in the analysis that you do, and it is important to be able to showcase the results in this manner. You will find that these methods, along with the textual writeup, are designed in a manner to refine and distill the data, making it easier for readers to glean interesting information out of that data, without having to go through and sort out the data on their own.

The data scientist is going to need to spend some time summarizing the data because this is going to be a critical step to the supporting arguments that they try to make with that data. And it is also important that we find ways to present this data in a manner that is understandable and clear, even to those who may not have the programming or technical knowledge do to the work, but who are using the data to help them create a successful business. You may also consider including the raw data as an appendix to your findings so that those who will use the information can quickly lookup all of the specifics that they need on their own.

When you are encountering some of these summarized conclusions and data, it is also important to view them in a more critical manner. Asking where the data is from is going to be an important step in this process, as is asking about what kind of sampling method was used in the first place to collect the data and even the size of the sample. Asking questions is going to ensure that the data is as organized as possible and that you know where the information is coming from, as well as any biases and slants that you need to be aware of.

For example, if you are going through this process and you are worried about there being a conflict of interest in the source of the data, then this is going to call into question some of the results that you are getting in the process. Likewise, data that is gathered from a small sample, or a sample that is not really random, can be of questionable utility as well. Reputable researchers are going to be able to provide you with the information that you need about the techniques they used to gather the information, the source of funding, and the point of why they collected the data in the beginning. This allows readers to think a bit more critically about the information before figuring out whether they are going to use it or not.

The Steps of a Data Analysis

There are a number of steps that need to come into play when we are ready to handle one of our own data analysis projects. Some of these steps are going to include:

1. Figuring out what business problem we would like to solve. Whether you have already done a

lot of the gathering that is needed of your chosen date, or you are just starting out and you want to know which type of data is the best to gather, you first need to go through and figure out which business problem you would like to solve. This can help to direct the way that this process goes, and ensures that you keep on track with the kind of information that you bring in.

2. Searching for the data that we want to work with. Once we have a good idea of the information that we need, and the business problem that we would like to solve, it is time for us to go through and look for the data. There are a number of places where we are able to find this data, such as in surveys, social media, and more, so going out and searching for it here is going to be the best way to gather it up and have it ready to work with on the later steps.

3. Cleaning and organizing our data. Since we are usually gathering our data from a lot of different places, and it is often going to come to us in a more unstructured form, it is always a good idea to go through and clean and organize that data. This will make it easier for us to putt that data

through the algorithm that we want to use and to make sure that it will all work out.

4. Getting rid of the outliers, duplicate information, and missing values. Outliers, missing values, and duplicate information in your set of data may not seem like a big deal, but they can definitely cause a number of problems with the results that you get. You need to look for these and then decide how you would like to proceed and handle some of them. This will ensure that the results you are working with are as secure and trustworthy as possible.

    a. In some cases, you may want to spend a bit of time taking a look at these outliers and deciding if they are important. If you see that there is a significant number of outliers that all converge together in a general area, this could be a breakthrough that you can use. It may help you to figure out a new niche to get into, or a new demographic that you could offer your product to. Not all outliers are going to be important, but paying a bit of attention and seeing if they have a similar place, they fall out of the normal is a good way to get ahead

5. Create a Python algorithm with machine learning We will spend some time looking at machine learning as we progress through this book, but in this step, we need to actually create the algorithm that is going to read through our data and give us the hidden insights and patterns that we are looking for. There are a number of algorithms that we are able to choose from, and sometimes experimenting and trying out a few options is going to be the best way to ensure that we are able to pick out the right one for our needs. You will also need to go through and train, before testing, the algorithm to make sure that it is able to learn along the way, and that it will be the right option for your needs.

6. Look over the insights and hidden patterns that were found in the data. The whole point of working with data analysis is to make sure that we can take a large amount of data and see what important insights are found in that information. The more that we study the data, and the better the algorithm we choose to work with, the easier it is to find the insights and the

hidden values that are inside of it. We can then use this to help us make better and more informed decisions.

7. Create a visualization: This is not a step that you should miss out on at all. These visuals are going to make it easier for those who are in charge of looking over the information to really see the connections and the relationships that show up in that data. This makes it easier for you to really figure out what the data is saying, and to figure out what decisions you should make based on that.

    a. There are a number of different types of visuals that you are able to work with, but the kind of data that you are sorting through, and the comparisons that you would like to make, are going to help you figure out the right one for your needs. Things like charts, graphs, and more will be the best options for helping you to get through this process as well.

As we can see, there are a lot of different parts that come with our data analysis and what we are able to do with this process. Taking the time to go through and learn more about the data analysis can make a big difference when it comes to how you will run your business. You will be able to use this in order to sort through all of the data you have collected and learned what is hidden inside. These can then be helpful when reaching out to your customers, working on marketing, figuring out how to open up a new niche to explore and more. But we first need to get ourselves through the process known as data analysis before we are able to use the data that we have been collecting.

The Benefits of Working with a Data Analysis

As you work with data analysis, it will not take long before you start to notice there are a number of benefits that come with this kind of process. That is why so many companies are ready and willing to jump on board with completing their own data analysis. They know that with the right kind of data, the right machine learning and Python algorithms, and more, they are able to go through and figure out a lot of different aspects of their business, and they can use this to help them get ahead in their industry as well. Some of the different benefits that you are able to enjoy when it is time to work with data analysis for your business will include:

Learn more about your customers. Learning more about your customers is a business practice that is never going to go out of style. Learning about how you can provide them with better customer service, how you can provide them with the best products, and even how you can work with recommendation systems, loyalty programs, and more in order to make the customer happier, while still increasing the amount of profit that you are able to make in the process as well. Working with your customers is so important to all businesses, and data analysis can help to show you the exact steps and process that you need to take in order to keep those customers coming back for more and spending more at your store as well.

Work on a stronger marketing campaign. When you have the ability to work with your customers and learn more about them, you will find that it is easier to market to these individuals. You can figure out which demographics are the best to market to, where to reach these individuals, and what they like to see in terms of marketing. With the Internet and other choices in technology that is available today, the number of methods that you can use in marketing is just going up all of the time. using data analysis to help you learn more about these customers and where they will see and respond to your marketing can be helpful in reaching more customers and reducing the waste that you get here.

Figure out a new demographic or niche to focus on. Sometimes the outliers that we find on our charts and in our information can actually tell us something. We may find that there is a significant distribution of the customers or another factor in one location that is not considered normal, and this is something that we need to focus on and look at closer than before. These outliers don't mean something all of the time, but in other cases, it does mean something and could open up some doors to a new demographic or market that we never focused on before. And if you are able to get there before the competition, and see success, it can help to open up new doors for the success of your business.

Pick out the right products to sell. In the past, releasing a new product could be risky. There were a number of steps that you could take in order to limit this risk a bit, but it was still a process that was not always as safe as a business would like. With the help of data analysis and going through a few steps before releasing the product in full to the market, can help make this a bit easier. By looking at the market, paying attention to customers, and other steps that are important to the data analysis process, you will be able to have more confidence that the products you release are going to do well.

Learn where waste is present and how to reduce it. No matter what industry you are in, it is possible that waste is holding you back a bit. There are a lot of places where waste can happen, and working with data analysis to figure out where this waste is coming from, and what we are able to do to reduce and even eliminate some of the waste is going to be a big part of helping to improve your bottom line. How nice would it be to decrease your costs and waste, while still being able to deliver the same kind of quality in your products to your customers? Think about how this would be able to improve your bottom line! And a good data analysis can help make this a reality for you.

As we can already see with this process, data analysis is going to take some time, and it may not be as quick and nice as some people will assume. But when we actually take the time to work with our raw data and pick out the right model and algorithms to use with it, the amount of information that we are able to learn from this is going to be outstanding. It may not be as easy and as fast as we would like, but those companies who have been willing to go through all of the steps that are necessary to do the data analysis for their own businesses have met with nothing but lots of success in the process.

Chapter 4: The Benefits and Negatives of Python for Data Analysis

With some knowledge about the Python language and what data analysis is all about, it is time for us to move onto how we are able to combine the two of these together in order to make sure that we can actually complete the data analysis and use that information to help promote the business and beat out the competition.

In this chapter, we are going to take a look at some of the benefits, as well as some of the negatives, that come with doing data analysis with Python. There are a lot of different programming languages out there that could handle some of the work that we want to do with our data analysis, but none of them are going to complete the job as well as Python can. With this in mind, let's take a look at some of the reasons why you may want to work with Python on your data analysis, and some of the drawbacks that you need to be on the lookout for in this process as well.

The Benefits

The first thing that we are going to take a look at is some of the benefits of using Python and why it is such a great option to use when you want to complete a project in data science. There may be a lot of other coding languages out there that we are able to work with, but none are going to provide us with quite the same mix of benefits and features as we can get with Python, and it won't take long to figure out why this is such a favorite when it comes to programmers and businesses who are working through the process of a data analysis. With this in mind, let's take a look at some of the benefits that come with working on a Python coding language, and of learning this language, in order to help complete your own data analysis in the process.

The first benefit is that the Python language, when it comes to comparison with some of the other coding languages out there, is pretty much as simple as it gets. The best part about learning this Python language is that you can be someone who has never done anything with Python in the past ever, and be completely new to the idea of programming, and still find that it is easy to grasp how coding work here.

The basics of working with Python are going to be easy to catch up on. You will find that the Python language is one that was designed with two basic things in mind; simplicity and readability. These are really unique features when it comes to working with this kind of language, and they are going to really bring us a lot of potentials when it is time to solve some big problems with our data in the data analysis. The simplicity of this language is what is going to make it one of the best options that we are able to work with when it comes to a coding language that can handle this kind of data analysis.

Another benefit that comes with the Python language is that it is fast and attractive. Apart from being pretty simple to work with, you will quickly notice that the Python code is leaner, and even better looking (as far as coding goes), than some of the other programming languages out there. For example, the Python code is going to take up about a third of the volume that we see with the Java code, and even less when it comes to the C++ code, and this is to perform the same task.

There are a number of reasons why the Python code is going to take up less room overall. For example, the use of common expressions, rather than relying on variable declarations and empty space rather than having the ugly brackets can help the flow of the Python code work better. It is also going to help to cut down on some of the work that you need to do when learning how to use the coding language. Overall, this coding language is going to save a lot of time and is a lot less taxing to the brain of those who are using them. And once you are able to get down some of the basics that come with the Python language, it makes working with your data analysis a lot easier.

With Python, we are going to find that the format of our data is not going to be as big of a deal. Python is going to work with all kinds of data. It is able to work with all of the different data formats and it is possible to take some of the different tables you have for SQL directly with this language. You are able to work with the JSON, Comma Separated value documents and the Python request library is going to make it easier for us to import the data that we want form different websites and then build up sets of data.

The data analysis library that we will often use for most of our data analysis is going to be known as Pandas, and this is able to hold onto a large amount of data, without issues from lagging and more. It is going to make the process of filtering, sorting, and then displaying the data as quickly as possible.

We may also see that the Python language is going to see huge growth in demand. While the demand for IT professionals in other areas has seen a bit of a decline in the past for years, you will find that the demand for those who are able to program with Python has steadily risen. Since Python has been able to prove itself as a great language for a lot of different things including data analytic programs and machine learning companies.

Companies that are going to center themselves around data are going to love Python skills and how this language can help them to get ahead. If you are able to prove that you have a stronghold with this coding language, you will be able to ride through the market right now and gain a lot of exposure with coding and more.

And finally, you will find that there is a vibrant community of lots of programmers that will provide you with some of the help and solutions that you are looking for as you go through some of your codings. You will find that there is a lot o helping hand whenever you are stuck with a problem that you are trying to figure out. Thanks to the fact that there are a lot of features to love about the Python language, we can see that the Python community has grown so big with a lot of members who are passionate and active.

What this means is that when you are working with the Python language, you are going to be able to find a lot of material that is around that will help you to figure out how to handle data science and data analysis and will help you to break out some of the deadlocks that are there. once you are able to learn some of the basics that are needed to use this language, which won't take too long to handle, you will be able to find the answers you need form this community as needed.

As we can see, we will find a lot of benefits when it is time to use the Python coding language to help out with some of our data analytics projects. There isn't a better option to work with than Python in order to help you to finish up the data analysis that you would like to work with.

The Negatives

Even though there are a lot of positives that come into play when we want to work with the Python language to help us with some of the data analysis we want to perform, but there are also going to be a few negatives that we need to take a closer look at as well. In this section, we are going to look at some of the reasons that some programmers will not work with the Python language when it comes to handling their data for data analysis and some of the things that you need to watch out for when working on data analysis.

First on the list is that the Python language is not going to have a good type of documentation. Some programmers do not like to work with this because they don't think that Python has good documentation. This is especially true when it is compared to some of the other programming languages out there, including Java and PHP. If you are working on a project that does need some of this good documentation assigned to it, then the Python language can push you back a bit on your work.

If you are working on a project that needs to focus a bit on something like statistical analysis, then the Python language may not be the right option for you. When it is compared to other options, such as R, you will find that Python is not going to be as thorough on its work as R for the statistical analysis. However, there have been some adjustments to this made recently, and it may not be long before Python is able to make up for this issue.

Another thing that we need to focus on is the learning curve. While the Python language is going to be an easy language to learn how to work with, and many beginners like to work with this one compared to some of the other options, there is going to be a little steeper learning curve compared to what we will see with other coding languages. The main reason for this is because the Python language has a lot more abilities and capabilities than what we are able to see with other coding languages, so the learning is going to take a bit longer. You just need to be prepared for this happening so that it doesn't come as a surprise.

In some situations, working with Python is not going to be strong enough for the program that you would like to develop. There are many times when this is not true, and learning Python is going to be worth your time. But then there are also times when it is going to lack the power, and you will need to add in a different coding language in order to help you get the work done with your models and algorithms.

Now, sometimes the library that you are using is going to be able to convert the Python language over to whatever language you want to use. For example, the TensorFlow library is going to convert the coding that you do in Python over to the C programming language. This makes it easier because you are able to write code in the Python coding language that you would like, and then the library is going to do the work that is necessary in order to change that Python code over into what we need for the algorithm.

In other cases, you will find that the library will not do this work for you. You will need to go through the process of learning another language or finding another type of model or algorithm to work with to get the work done. This can make it a bit more difficult for a beginner and can make things frustrating when it is time to do some of the codings. The good news with this one though is that Python will be able to handle most of the work that you want to do, so this shouldn't be a big problem all of the time.

As we can see, there are a lot of times when we are going to find the Python language as a useful option to get things done with our data analysis. But then there are also some times when this may not be the right language to help us get some work done that we want to handle. It is important to know when to bring in the Python language, and when we need to look for a different model or a different type of programming language to help us get things done. Knowing when this needs to happen can make a world of difference in how well our data analysis goes.

Chapter 5: A Look At Databases and How Python Can Help

Python is one of the best options to work with when it is time to handle some of our database programmings. Data forms are going to be a very important part of the data analysis process. From the number of people who are in an airport to the count of stationery that is found in a bookstore, everything today that we record in the form of digital files called databases.

These may sound complicated, but they are nothing more than a list of information that is electronic. Some of the databases that you are going to encounter will be simply because they are designed to handle some smaller lists or smaller tasks. And then there are some that are more powerful because they are designed to help out with big data. All of them, whether they are simple or more complicated, are going to have the same commonalities and will perform a similar function with each other. With this in mind, we are going to take a look at these databases, and some of the codes that we can use in order to get started making and working with our own databases in Python.

The Relational Database

The first thing that we need to take a look at is the relational database. This is going to consist of one or more tables of information that we are able to use. The rows in the table are going to be known as records and the columns are going to be attributes or fields. A database that has two or more of these related tables will be known as a relational database. The main idea that comes with this is that the data is going to be broken down, so it becomes a common theme, with one of the tables dedicated to describing the records of each theme.

There are a few different parts that are going to come with the relational database as you set it up. We are going to start with the database tables. Each table that is in one of these databases is going to come with one or more columns, and then each of the columns will be assigned a specific type of data. This could include something like a date, a sequence of characters to hold onto the text or even an integer number. There are a few important characteristics that are found in the tables of these databases and they will include:

1. There is not going to be any significance found in the order of the rows or the columns.
2. Each row is going to contain one, and no more, value for every column you have.
3. Each value is going to have a given column is going to be the same type.
4. Each table in the database should hold onto information about a specific thing, including something like customers, products, or employees.

When we go through and design our database in this manner, it is going to help to eliminate the number of inconsistencies and redundancies that show up in your database. For example, both the accounts and sales payable departments are going to look up information about the customers. in a relational database, the information about customers is only going to be put in once, in a table that both of these departments are able to access when needed.

Another thing that we need to take a look at is the primary and foreign keys. These both are going to help us to define the relational structure of the database. These keys are going to enable each row in the table to be identified and define the relationships that are found between the tables. The different types of keys that we are able to work with here include:

1. Primary keys: This is going to be able to uniquely identify each record that is in the table. It is a column, and sometimes a set of columns, that is going to allow each row in the table to be uniquely identified. No two rows in your table with a primary key can come with the same primary key value.

2. Foreign key: This is going to be a field in the relational table that will match with the primary key column of another table.

Database Management Systems

The database management system, known as DBMS, is a software that interacts with end-users, applications, and the database on its own in order to capture and analyze the data. The DBMS is going to be used for the Rational databases in many cases as well. The RDBMS, or Relational Database Management Systems, are going to used SQL, a declarative language for taking the data and manipulating it, in order to access the database that they want to work with. There are a number of different types of RDBMS that we are able to work with include SQLite, Microsoft Access PostgreSQL, Microsoft SQL Server, MySQL, and Oracle to name a few.

One of these databases that we need to explore is known as SQLite. This is a relational database management system that has been designed to work with the SQL language. This database has also been optimized to use with a variety of small environments, including mobile phones and other small applications. There are a lot of things to enjoy about this process including the fact that it is transactional, zero-configuration serverless, and self-contained.

Another thing to like with this is that SQLite is very lightweight and fast, and you are able to store the entire database is stored in a single disk file as well. It is built to be used for speed and simplicity compared to a hosted client-server relational database including MySQL. It is going to sacrifice sophistication a bit, but this ensures that it is able to help with the utility to get more done. You will find that the queries that are done with this one is going to be pretty similar to some of the other SQL calls that you are used to working with.

Creating Our Python SQLite Model

With some of that information behind us, it is time to take a look at how we are able to integrate SQLite with Python using a module from Python known as sqlite3. You will not have to go through and install this module on its own, because it is already going to be bundled up with any version of Python that is Python 2.5 or higher.

However, it is also a good idea to install the DB Browser for SQLite before you get started. this browser is something that you are able to download off the official page pretty quickly. This is a high quality, open-source and visual tool that is going to help you easily create, design, and edit the files of the database in a format that is compatible with SQLite as we would like. This is going to make it easier to see the database being created and edited in real-time.

With this in mind, we are going to take a look at some of the steps that we need to take in order to get started with this module. The first step is to connect ourselves to the database. To do this, we need to open up any IDE for Python that we want to use. We are able to work with any kind of IDE< and even the Jupyter Notebook is going to work just fine for this project as well if that is what you would like to work with. In general, the only thing that we need to do before we can perform an operation in this database through this Python module is to open a connection to the SQLite database file. The commands that we need to use to complete this first step will include:

```
import sqlite3
conn = sqlite3.connect('my_database.sqlite'
)cursor = conn.cursor()
print("Opened database successfully")
```

The code that we wrote out above in Python is going to be a simple way to connect to our existing database using the object of conn in order to help us do the connection. Now, if you are trying to connect with a database that is not in existence yet, then this is the time where it will be created. And when the creation of that database is done, you are going to get the object of the database returned. A cursor object is going to be the interface to the database, one that is going to allow us to run any of the queries that we want with SQL on the database.

If we have done the above code in the proper manner, and if all goes well, we are going to see the line "Opened database successfully". From here, we can open up and view the new database that we created in our DB browser from before. Right now we should see a brand new database that is named my_database.sqlite. Right now, this is going to be an empty database because we have not had the time to put anything in it yet.

Before we go any further with this one, there are a few more things that we need to mention when working on this part of the code. If we have decided that we are finished with the operations that are found in our file on the database, we then have to make sure that we have closed up that connection. This is done with a simple code of "conn.close()."

And if we did go through our other database and performed an operation on that database, any kind of operation other than sending in the queries that were needed, it is time to go through and commit those changes. We are able to commit them with the .commit() method, and it needs to be done before we decide to close the connection as we did above. The coding that we would need to have to finish this off includes:

```
conn.commit()
conn.close()
```

We need to remember here that it is important to commit the current transaction. Since the default of this process is not to commit automatically for us, it is important to call this method after every transaction that is able to modify the data for the tables that are working on storage engines that are transactional. If you do not call up this method, anything that you performed since the last call to commit is not going to save and it is not going to be visible from the other connections on the database.

Now that we are done with that step, it is time to move on to the second step of our process. Here, we are going to focus on what is needed in order to create the table that we want to work with. We are going to work on creating a table in the database that we created in the last step. The code that we need to use to make this happen will include the following:

```
cursor.execute('''CREATE TABLE SCHOOL
      (ID INT PRIMARY KEY     NOT NULL,
      NAME            TEXT    NOT NULL,
      AGE             INT    NOT NULL,
      ADDRESS         CHAR(50),
      MARKS           INT);''')cursor.close()
```

With this, we have been able to create the table that
we need within that previously created database. Here
we were able to create a table that includes a few
different fields including ID, Name, Age, Address, and
Marks, and the table is known as school. We also took
some time to designate as ID Primary Key and then
closed up the connection.

Having the table in our database is not the only step
that we need to undertake when we are working
through this process. We also need to put some
information into the table so that we are able to work
on it and see what results are in our data. We are now
going to take some time to insert the records of the
students into the table that we just created. The code
that we need to use in order to make this happen with
Python and our own database includes:

```python
import sqlite3conn =
sqlite3.connect('my_database.sqlite')
cursor = conn.cursor()cursor.execute("INSERT INTO
SCHOOL (ID,NAME,AGE,ADDRESS,MARKS) \
    VALUES (1, 'Rohan', 14, 'Delhi', 200)");
cursor.execute("INSERT INTO SCHOOL
(ID,NAME,AGE,ADDRESS,MARKS) \
    VALUES (2, 'Allen', 14, 'Bangalore', 150 )");
cursor.execute("INSERT INTO SCHOOL
(ID,NAME,AGE,ADDRESS,MARKS) \
    VALUES (3, 'Martha', 15, 'Hyderabad', 200 )");
cursor.execute("INSERT INTO SCHOOL
(ID,NAME,AGE,ADDRESS,MARKS) \
    VALUES (4, 'Palak', 15, 'Kolkata',
650)");conn.commit()
conn.close()
```

With the coding that we did above, and if everything
fits into the right spot as it should, you are going to
have a full table inside of your database. Go ahead
and execute this part of the program and see whether
the different parts fall in the right spot and that you
will be able to see that the ages all in the right spot,
the name, address, the marks.

Now that the table is created, there are going to be times when we want to pull up certain parts of the table or find certain information in it as well. That is why the next task that we want to spend some time on is going to be how we can select records off the table. Let's say that we would like to be able to select some particular records from the table. Maybe we just want to look at the name column or even a specific name in the table. This is something that we can easily handle when we work with the Select command. The code that we are able to use in order to make this happen includes:

```
import sqlite3conn =
sqlite3.connect('my_database.sqlite')cursor =
conn.cursor()for row in cursor.execute("SELECT id,
name, marks from SCHOOL"):print("ID = ", row[0])
    print("NAME = ", row[1])
    print("MARKS = ", row[2], "\n")conn.commit()
conn.close()
```

Go ahead and type this into your Jupyter Notebook or another compiler or IDE that you are using, and then see what the results are. If you do it right, it should just up the ID, Name, and Marks of the right person within the table that you were able to create.

This is not the only thing that we are able to do with that table that we just went through and created. It is also possible to do a few other tasks on the table as well, such as updating some of the records that are found in your table. Maybe you find that you put the mark of the person down wrong, or they changed addresses, and you want to make some modifications to ensure that the table is up to date.

Now we are going to take some time to learn how to work with the Update command in order to help us update any record within our table. We are also going to use the coding that is necessary to, after the update, fetch and then display the updated records from the School table that we already created. For this one, we are going to work on updating the marks for Martha from 200 to 250, and then have the records fetched for us. The code that we need to use to make these marks change will include the following:

```
import sqlite3conn =
sqlite3.connect('my_database.sqlite')
cursor = conn.cursor()conn.execute("UPDATE SCHOOL
set MARKS = 250 where ID = 3")conn.commit()for
row in cursor.execute("SELECT id, name, address,
marks from SCHOOL"):print("ID = ", row[0])
    print("NAME = ", row[1])
    print("MARKS = ", row[2], "\n")conn.commit()
conn.close()
```

The next thing that we are going to take a look at
when it comes to handling some of the databases that
we want to take care of within our coding is how we
are able to delete some of the different parts that
come within your table. We are able to use the
operation of Delete to make sure that we can take
away any of the records that are found on our Table
for School.

Let us say that Allen has left the school and isn't going to come back at all. Maybe we want to go through and delete Allen's records from the database since he is no longer going to the school and we don't need to keep track of all of the information and the different stuff about him. We are going to first work on fetching the details of all the records of all the students that go to this school and are on the table. The coding that we need in order to delete the different parts of the table that we want will include:

```
import sqlite3conn =
sqlite3.connect('my_database.sqlite')
cursor = conn.cursor()conn.execute("DELETE from
SCHOOL where ID = 2")conn.commit()for row in
cursor.execute("SELECT id, name, address, marks
from SCHOOL"):print("ID = ", row[0])
    print("NAME = ", row[1])
    print("ADDRESS = ", row[2])
    print("MARKS = ", row[3], "\n")conn.commit()
conn.close()
```

These are some of the different things that we are able to work on in order to handle some of the different parts that come with your database. There are a lot of times when data analysis is going to gather up the information that creates their models and helps them to make good business decisions from a database. This is one of the best ways to organize the data that we have and can be a great way to fix any problems that are found in the data, such as duplicates and missing values. Once the data is organized inside of that database, we are able to take it and organize it in a manner that is easy to understand for some of our Python models and machine learning algorithms.

The topics that we went through in this chapter will make sure that we can create our database and a table, that we can input the information that we need, and that we can then change or add any information that is needed. This can take us a long way when it is time to handle our data and get it prepared for everything that we need to do with data science and our own data analysis.

Chapter 6: An Introduction to Pandas

The first thing that we need to take a look at while we are working with our data analysis is an introduction to the Python library known as Pandas. There are a lot of great libraries out there that are able to combine together with the Python library and ensure that we are going to be able to handle a lot of the different parts that come with data science and completing data analysis. With this said, the Pandas library is one of the best options to work with, and when we can use it in the proper manner, it is easier than ever to really take control over our project and see the results that we want.

With this in mind, we need to take some time to learn more about the Pandas library and what is going to come with it along the way. to start, Pandas is going to be a library that is available through Python. The point of using this is to make sure that we can see a faster amount of processing with data analysis, data cleaning, and data pre-processing. Pandas are going to work so well because it is built upon a few other libraries, including NumPy.

Basically, when NumPy and Pandas get together, they will both gain some superpowers that can make them easier to work with overall. There are a lot of neat features that you will be able to enjoy with the Pandas library, and with the NumPy library when the two combine together that you are not going to see when they are on their own.

At some point, you may have heard about something that is known as a data-frame. This is a pretty common term when we are talking about all of the things that you are able to do with machine learning. The term data frames though are going to come from Pandas. Pandas is able to take those data frames and helps us to create our own with ease. This can be helpful when we are working with data science overall.

Pandas is an easy library to work with, even though it is something that may seem like it is really complicated to work with. You will find that many programmers are going to compare it to working with Excel sheets. A lot of the features that you are able to find with an Excel sheet is going to be available in pandas as well. Of course, though, you are going to find that the Pandas library is going to have a lot of other features that make it a smarter choice to work with than what we see with just relying on an Excel sheet.

Before you work on installing this to your computer, you need to make sure that not only is the Python language set up and ready to use, but that the NumPy language is there as well. Pandas are going to build off some of the work that you are able to do with NumPy, so if it is not there, then the program is not going to work the way that you would like. Make sure to download these together in one if you need or get NumPy set up and ready to go when you are read.

With this in mind, you may be worried about how to work with Pandas, whether it is going to be too hard to handle as a beginner and some of the different ways that we are able to work with the Pandas library to get our data analysis done. Let's take a look at some of the different tasks that we are able to see when we are working with the Pandas library.

What Pandas Can Help With

Now that we know a bit more about the Pandas library, it is important that we take some time to learn more about what the Pandas library is able to help us out with along the way. While there are a lot of different types of libraries and extensions that work with the Python library and can handle your data analysis, the Pandas library is considered one of the best. This is because the Pandas library is set up in order to handle all of the different parts of the process, from gathering up the data that you need to use in this process all the way to help you create some of the important visuals that will help us to get the work done.

This is part of why the Pandas library is one of the best ones out there to help us get some of our work done. Learning how this library is supposed to work, and some of the different steps that go with it make it a very powerful library to focus on as well. With this in mind, let's take a quick look at some of the different things that the Pandas library is able to help us out with when we get started with our own data analysis.

The first thing that the Pandas library is able to help us out with is loading and then saving the data that we would like to work on within our analysis. As a business, there is a wealth of information out there that we are able to work with. But it is important to know what kind of data we are looking for, and then figure out the proper method to gather up that data and store it until we are ready to complete our own analysis.

This is a process that can take some time and is sometimes frustrating because we want to learn what insights are in that information as soon as possible, however, it is a process, and the Pandas library is able to help us get it all done. We can use Pandas to help us go out there and gather the data that we want to work with, and even to save and store the data until we are ready to move on and use that data for some other purposes.

From there we are able to move on to viewing and inspecting the data that we have. Just because we have collected a bunch of data does not mean that it is going to work well for all of our needs and there are times when we will need to drop some of the data and not work with it. With a bit of searching, it is likely that we will be able to eliminate some of the data that is not going to be that necessary and focus more on the data that is needed to help us meet our business goals.

Selecting the data and figuring out which kind that we want to work within the analysis is important as well. One of the things that you will notice as a lot easier when it is time to work with this library over some of the others is that selecting the data that you would like to look over and compare is going to be easier than selecting a value from a dictionary or a list. This library has it set up so that you can easily select a column or another part of the code or database that you would like to work with and ensure that it comes up.

The way that you determine what kind of information that you would like to compare is going to be based on what you plan to use that data for. There are many business problems that we are able to solve with the help of data analysis, but we have to pick the one that is the most critical, or at least the one that is going to help us out the most first, and then move on from there. Selecting the data that meets up with the business problem that we want to solve should be the logical next step.

From here, we are going to move on to organizing and sorting through all of the data that we want to handle. There are a number of ways that we are able to handle this part, and we can organize the data with the help of filter, sort, and groupby. All of these are going to be slightly different, but when you know what kind of information you want to work with, and how it is supposed to work together, you will find that it is easier to make this happen.

Before you are able to go through and finish with your algorithm though, and even before we can send the data in through the model, we need to spend some time cleaning our data. Since most companies are going to spend their time collecting data from a wide variety of sources, and most of this data is going to be unstructured and kind of unorganized, data cleaning is going to be an important step.

If you have gone through and worked with some of the other parts that we talked about above, then you will only need to complete the data cleaning on some of the data that you actually plan to use in the process. This is an important step because it organizes some of the unstructured data, gets rid of the outliers that are going to make too much nice, helps to fill in the missing values, and will make sure that some of the duplicate content is taken care of so it doesn't mess with the answers and insights that you are able to get from your data.

From here, we are able to move on to working with the data analysis and actually creating the model that we want to use. This is where the Python language is going to shine. It is able to combine with machine learning to create some of the best algorithms and models that, after the training and the testing phases, are able to go through and read through our data and provide us with the hidden insight and patterns that are there.

These algorithms are diverse, and there are many different ones that we are able to focus on using. You will find that options like decision trees, random forests, clustering, K-Nearest Neighbors, support vector machines, and even neural networks are going to be a great option to work with as needed. These can all come into use based on the kind of data that we are working with and how we want to learn from it.

Taking your time creating the right algorithm and figuring out how to make it more accurate can be important. You will learn that over time, the more that you train and test your algorithm, the easier it is to work with. What this means is that while the algorithm may not be as accurate as you would like in the beginning, with some time and perseverance in the process, you will be able to help the algorithm learn, and the accuracy is going to go right up.

No matter what kind of algorithm you decide to work on when it is time to do an analysis, you have to set aside some data for training, and some for testing. The training set is going to spend time teaching the algorithm how you would like it to behave, giving it examples of what is expected and what output should go with each input. Then, after you have had some time to feed in a lot of examples like this to the algorithm or model, it can be tested.

During the testing phase, the model is going to receive the input, but no output will come with it. The point is to see how much the model was able to learn along the way and how accurate it is. The more data that you are able to feed through the model that you created, and the more times you can do some training and testing, the more accurate these models are going to become.

And the final thing that we are able to use the Pandas library to help us out with here is how to work with the visuals. These visuals are very important, and it is not a step that we should try to skip out on. Instead, it is something very important and we need to make sure that once we see some of the valuable insights and predictions that come with our data, we are able to switch them around and turn them into a visual.

These visuals help us to better see some of the complex relationships that show up in our data. For most people, looking over a chart and seeing what patterns are present is much easier and faster to understand than reading through a spreadsheet or a report and hoping to make sense of the information that is there. A written report certainly has its place, but so do the visuals.

You will find that the Pandas library is going to provide us with a lot of opportunities to work with these visuals and handle all of the parts that come with it as well. And when we add in the Matplotlib extension, we will find that it is easier than ever to actually handle some of these parts and make some of the best visuals to aid us in our data analysis.

As we can see here there are a lot of different things that the Pandas library is able to help us out with. When it combines together with the Python library, you will find that it is going to be really strong, and is one of the best ways to ensure that we are able to handle our data science project and complete the analysis that we want to get done. Without Pandas, handling our data analysis is going to be much harder, and it is not going to work the way that we want. But with Pandas, things get a lot easier to work with overall, and it will be easier than you think to get started with your own data analysis.

Chapter 7: How to Set Up and Install the Pandas Library

Now that we have a bit more information about the Pandas library and how we are able to work with it, it is time for us to learn how to set up and work with the Pandas library. You will find that the Pandas library is one of the best data analysis libraries, and it is going to take some time to handle all of the different aspects of the data analysis process. This is one of the reasons why we need to take some time to download this library and get it set up to work with Python so that you can handle your work with data analysis.

With this in mind, it is time for us to move on and learn how we are able to set up and install the Pandas library on your system. This is a simple process that we are able to work with, and it is not meant to be complicated. But we do need to take a look at some of the different steps that are needed in order to load and then save Pandas and get it ready to use on your system.

How to Install Pandas

The first thing that we are going to take a look at is the steps, and the coding, that we need to do in order to get Pandas ready to go and installed on our system. To make sure that we are able to use Pandas, it needs to first be installed on our computer. We are going to make the assumption that you went through the steps needed earlier in order to get Python all set up and ready to go with your system, so that will save some of the time and energy that we need to use for this process right now.

To get us started with this, we need to check what version of Python we are working with. If you decided to download Python recently, then it is likely that you are working with a version of Python 3, and that will work just fine with Pandas. But if you have been working with Python for some time and installed it a long time ago on your system, then it is important to check which version. Pandas works with any version of Python that is Python 2.7 or higher so make sure that you have a version that fits or updates which type of Python you are working with.

Once we are certain that we are working with a new enough version of the Python library to get the work done, it is time to take a look at some of the libraries that are available to work with as well. We have to make sure that the NumPy library is present on our system because this library is going to be able to work with the NumPy arrays. Without NumPy on our system already, the Pandas library is not going to do what we would like.

We also have some optional libraries that we are able to work within this library as well. The Matplotlib library is a great option, especially when it is time to work with some plotting or with a few of the visuals that are helpful with our data analysis. Because of these different options that we want to work with, one of the easiest methods that you are able to work with here is to install all of the necessary and optional libraries needed to make Pandas work with through a package like the Anaconda distribution.

This is a great option to work with because it helps us to go through and get all of those libraries in one place. Rather than having to go through and download all of these extensions and libraries one by one, we are able to go through and install them at once through the Anaconda distribution, or through another similar kind of distribution as well. This will allow us to download all of this to Windows, Mac, and Linux versions. If you would like to install it in a different manner, then we are going to go through the steps and the coding that will help you to get all of this done.

To make sure that we are able to get Pandas to work on your system and to make sure that it is going to be compatible with your Python IDE means that we need to import this library first. Importing the Pandas library is easier than you may think in the beginning, because it just means that we are going to load the library into the memory, and then it is there for you to bring out and work with any time that you would like. The code that we need to use in order to import Pandas to our system is to run with the following code:

```
import pandas as pd
import numpy as np
```

Usually, we need to make sure that we are able to go through and add in the second part of both lines above in order to make it easier to bring up some of the parts that we want to do with coding later on. For example, with the pd part, we are able to write out something like pd.command rather than having to go through and write out pandas. command each time that we would like to use this.

As we can see above as well, we are able to import the NumPy library. Remember that we talked about how this library is going to be an important one to work with because Pandas needs to have the NumPy arrays around in order to finish some of the scientific computing that comes with our data analysis and machine learning.

At this point, if you were able to go through the process properly and everything is ready, you can start to work with the Pandas library. Remember, you will need to use that two-line code from above each time that you start up the Python IDE, whether it is a Spyder file, a Jupyter Notebook, or something else similar along the way. this ensures that the compiler and the Notebook know that you would like to use that to see the best results with your work.

Chapter 8: What is Machine Learning and How It Fits In

Any time that we are ready to handle data analysis, it is important that we take some time to explore the basics of machine learning. It is impossible to conduct a good data analysis without talking about and using machine learning. Machine learning is able to handle some of the different tasks that are needed to take all of that data we have collected and actually create some good insights and predictions out of the hidden patterns that are inside.

We will also need to use machine learning, along with the help of codes that are written out in Python, to help us get started with some of our models and algorithms. These algorithms can be trained to take some or all of the data that we have available and sort through it automatically for us. This is how your business is able to go through and get those hidden insights and patterns out of the data, without having to do it manually.

With this in mind, we need to take a look at some of the basics that come with machine learning. This will help us to see what machine learning is really all about, how it works, and how we are going to come to rely on it when we handle our own data analysis.

The first thing that we need to take some time to explore though is the basics of machine learning. Machine learning is just going to be a method of data analysis that is able to automate some of the analytical model building that we need to deal with. It is going to be one of the branches that come with artificial intelligence and it will be based on the idea that a system is able to take data and learn from it. This system is also able to use that data to help it identify problems and make decisions. And all of this can be done with little to no intervention from humans.

Because of some of the new technologies in computing that are out there, the machine learning that we are likely to see today is not going to be the same as the machine learning that may have been used in the past. Instead, it is born from pattern recognition, along with a theory that says how a computer is able to learn anything that we want, without needing to be performed to that specific task in the first place.

In the beginning, researchers who were interested in some of the different parts of artificial intelligence wanted to get started by seeing if a computer or another system was able to learn from the data that we tried to present to it. The neat thing here is that machine learning is going to have an iterative aspect that will help it to learn. This is important because as the models are exposed to more and more data over time, they will be able to make the necessary adaptations along the way.

What happens with machine learning is that the model is trained to adapt and to learn as needed along the way. these models are going to learn from some of the computations that happened earlier, and the hopes are that they are going to come up with some results and decisions that are repeatable and reliable. It is a science that may not be brand new, but it is gaining a lot of popularity as time goes on.

While a lot of the algorithms that are available for machine learning have been around for a number of years, the ability out there to automatically apply some big and complex calculations over to the big data that we want to use, and do this in a faster method each time that we do it, is something that is more recently developed. However, even though it is recent does not mean that a lot of companies have not taken the time to learn more about it and how it is able to work for their needs.

We are able to see examples of machine learning everywhere we look and as more and more businesses start to hear about data analysis, big data, and some of the other buzz words that come with machine learning, it is likely that we are going to see even more of these machine learning innovations in the future.

The Importance of Machine learning

The next thing that we need to take a look at here is why machine learning is seen as such an important thing today. There is a lot of interest out there when it comes to machine learning and all of the things that we have talked about in this guidebook, and it is definitely growing along with things like data mining and data analysis. Things like the growing amount and types of data, the idea that we are able to process things faster and for less money, and that it is easier to store our data until we need it to have all come into play when it is time to work with machine learning.

All of these different things mean that it is very much possible for us to quickly and then automatically produce some of the models that we need. Today, and in the future, we will find that these models are able to handle and analyze ever-growing and more complex types of data while providing us with results that are very accurate and can be presented and delivered faster than ever. And the best part is that this can be done to scale, allowing us the ability to do all o this with however much data we would like.

In addition, we will find that when we are able to take the time to build up precise models, the organization is going to have a better chance of finding opportunities that are more profitable and will put their business ahead in no time. it is even a great method to use when it is time to avoid some of the unknown risks that could face the business in the future.

Do I Really Need Machine Learning?

You may be spending some time looking through this chapter and learning a bit about machine learning, but still, feel confused as to why you would want to spend your time actually using machine learning. It may seem like something out of a book or a movie. Is it really possible to use some coding, even the basic Python code, in order to create algorithms and models that can learn? Is it actually possible for us to take our data and figure out the insights that are in it just by presenting it to a machine learning algorithm?

It may sound like something that is not reality and something from a Sci-Fi movie, but this is definitely the way that the world is taking us right now. By this, we are talking about the wide variety of entities and companies who are already jumping on board with machine learning and using it for some of their needs.

When you spend some time with machine learning, it is not going to take long before you start to see that any industry and any company, who spends time working with data and collecting it will be able to find some kind of value when they work with machine learning as well. And if you plan to do anything with data analysis, and sort through your data to figure out the best course of action to take on a regular basis, then machine learning is definitely something that you need to spend your time with overall.

With this said, there are a lot of companies in many different industries who are relying on machine learning to help them get ahead. Some of the different industries and companies who are already working with this kind of machine learning to help them out with their data analysis will include:

1. Financial services: There are so many companies within the financial sector who will be able to benefit from using machine learning to help them reach their goals. They will find that machine learning is able to help them figure out who to loan money to, how much to loan out in credit cards, who is the most likely to pay back,

and how to avoid things like money laundering and fraud.

2. Healthcare: This is another industry where we are going to see a lot of big changes when it comes to how they are able to use machine learning. This is an industry that is fast paced, with very little room for error, but it is likely to see a gap in the number of people they are able to employ over the next few years. Some of the models and algorithms that we are able to create with machine learning can help to solve a few of these problems as well.

   a. For example, some of the technology that is used with machine learning is already helping out these industries and providing them with a way to better serve their patients. This technology is already found in some areas like helping complete surgeries, helping to answer questions for patients, and making it easier for a doctor to complete a look over some charts and tests.

3. Oil and gas: There are also a lot of ways that this kind of industry will be able to benefit when it is time to work with machine learning. Some o

these are going to include streamlining some of the distribution that the company is using in order to ensure that the process is more efficient and doesn't cost as much, learning how to predict when the sensors of the refinery are going to break, analyzing some of the minerals that are found in the ground, and finding new sources of energy to work with. The number of machine learning use cases for this kind of industry is vast and is likely to grow in the future so it is definitely something that these professionals should take a look at.

4. Government: Government agencies, including those who are in charge of utilities and other parts of public safety, may be able to find machine learning as a useful tool. They are able to take in data to figure out how to keep others as safe as possible in the long run, and it can even come into play when it is time to help the government detect fraud and minimize the amount of identity theft that is happening.

5. Retail: This is one of those industries where it may seem like machine learning is not going to matter, but when we stop and think about all of the information and data that these companies

are able to gather and store about their customers, it is no wonder that they want to get in on some of the work with data analysis and machine learning as well. These retail stores are able to use this information to help them market to their customers better, provide a better recommendation system, pick out which products to sell, and more.

6. Transportation: And finally, we need to take some time to look at how the transportation industry is going to be able to use machine learning. A good way to look at this is that this industry is going to analyze data to help identify some of the trends and patterns that are found inside. This is able to help us make our routes more efficient and can be good for predicting the potential problems to increase the amount of efficiency that is found in the company.

As we can see, there are already a lot of industries and companies who have seen the value that machine learning is able to provide, and who have decided to jump on board and see how this is able to benefit them as well. Whether you are still considering adding some machine learning to your big data and seeing what insights are in that data or not, you can definitely benefit when it comes to implementing some machine learning in as well.

Machine Learning Methods

While we are here, we need to take a bit of time to look at some of the different types of machine learning algorithms. Each of these is going to be important because they are able to handle a different type of problem that we would like to handle in our algorithms and with our data. We are going to be able to bring up each one based on what we are trying to do with the data at hand.

The first kind of machine learning technique that we are going to work with is known as supervised machine learning. This is a basic type of machine learning technique where we are going to present the algorithm with the input, and its known output at the same time. This is a good method to use because it ensures that the algorithm is able to learn based on the examples that are present.

We can think of this one like what happens when a teacher is trying to show a new topic to their class. They are not just going to list out a few sentences about it and then expect that the students are going to know what they should do or what the right and wrong answers are. Instead, the teacher will then present some information to the students, and some examples that go along with it so that they can actually learn.

This is similar to what we are going to do with supervised machine learning. This is set up to help us to work with an algorithm that is able to learn based on the input and output that we are able to provide to it. This takes some more time but can speed up the learning process because the algorithm knows exactly what examples are going to be the most useful here. A good example of this is if a bank would like to teach the algorithm of how to respond and notice fraudulent charges. The data scientist would feed in a lot of examples of past fraudulent activity so that the algorithm is able to learn about it along the way.

Then we are able to work with semi-supervised machine learning. This one is going to be used for a lot of the same kinds of applications as we talked about above. But you will find that the difference is there is a combination of unlabeled and labeled data that is used for training. For the most part, we are going to use a small amount of labeled data that is mixed in with the huge amount of unlabeled data that we would like to focus on.

The reason that we use this one is that we like the idea of working with labeled data, but it is expensive and hard for the company to gather and work with all that labeled data. The unlabeled data is easier to find and a lot less expensive, so the data scientist is going to do a combination of the two in order to still get a bit of both worlds.

We will find that this kind of learning is going to be used with a lot of the different machine learning projects that we want to handle including prediction, classification, and regression. This kind of learning is going to be used when we find that the costs that come with finding some labeled data are going to be too high for us to use only labeled data in the process. But it is still important to have some kind of labeled data present in the process as well.

The third type of machine learning that we are able to work with is going to be known as unsupervised machine learning. This one is going to be a little bit different than what we were talking about with the two other options above, mainly because it is going to not use historical labels and it is not going to be given all of the examples that we did with supervised machine learning. The system is not going to be given the right answer from the programmer when it is being set up.

The algorithm with this one needs to figure out what is being shown, all on its own. The goal with it is that we want the algorithm to explore the data and then figure out what the hidden pattern or structure is within this. Unsupervised learning is going to work the best on transactional data so that is the place where we are going to see it the most.

For example, this kind of learning is going to be able to take a look at some of the customers we are working with and then identify the segments of those customers who have similar attributes. We are then able to treat these customers the same when we work on a marketing campaign. There are a lot of great machine learning algorithms that we are able to use that fit into this, and learning how to make these works, and picking out an algorithm that fits with unsupervised machine learning can be a useful part of your data analysis.

Reinforcement learning is going to be the final type of machine learning that we are able to work with. This one, to those who have not spent a lot of time learning about machine learning and what it is about, may assume that unsupervised learning and reinforcement learning are the same things. And from the outside, they do appear to be similar. But we are going to spend some time looking at the differences and why reinforcement learning is going to be considered a little bit different.

When we are talking about reinforcement learning, there are going to be a few things that come to mind including gamin, robotics, and navigation. With reinforcement kind of learning, the algorithm is going to be in charge of discovering, through a process of trial and error, which actions are going to provide it with some of the best rewards in the process.

There are three main components including the agent, the environment, and the actions that need to come together to help us figure out how to work with this algorithm. The objective overall, as we work through with this, is for the agent to make sure that they are always choosing the right action to get the biggest reward in the end.

How Does Machine Learning Work?

Working with machine learning is a more complex option to handle, but the steps seem easy to work with it. To help us get the most out of this machine learning though, we need to make sure that we not only pick out the algorithms with the right processes and tools. When you are able to combine together the data mining and statistics that come with data analysis, new architectural advances to ensure that the models we use not only work, but they run as fast as possible.

Medium and large businesses are able to use data analysis and machine learning to help them reach their customers and stay as successful as possible. But this doesn't mean that they want to sit around and wait forever in order to get that data set up and ready to go. This is why we need to make sure that the tools and processes are paired with the right algorithm are able to keep up with them, and that they will not have to wait around to see the results. This doesn't mean that machine learning is going to be an instant solution and that it doesn't take some time. but we need to make sure that it all fits together and that we are able to get some good results out of it without having to wait months or years to get it done.

So, the first thing that we need to have in order to get machine learning to do the work that we would like is the right algorithm. Most of these algorithms are going to run thanks to the Python coding language, which makes them one of the perfect ways to handle all of that data. But you will quickly find that when you are working with data analysis and all of the parts that need to come with this, you will find that there are a lot of different algorithms that we are able to pick from.

The type of algorithm that we are able to work with will depend on what you would like to see happen with some of your data. The business question that you decide to ask to form the beginning and the business problem that you would like to have answered will help you pick out which algorithm you would like to work with. Some of the different types of algorithms that we are able to work with will include things like decision trees and random forests, neural networks, support vector machines, clustering and more.

We also need to make sure that we have the right tools in place to handle some of the work that we would like to get done. This is going to ensure that the algorithms we are trying to work with are going to show up where they need to and that everything is going to fall into place without a lot of issues along the way. Some of the different tools that we may want to work with when it is time to handle our own data analysis will include:

1. A comprehensive amount of management for our data, and high-quality data.

2. GUIS to help us to build up the models that we want to use with machine learning. And a good process flow.
3. A way to compare some of the different models that come with machine learning, so we have a better chance of figuring out which one is the best for our needs.
4. Interactive exploration of any data that we want to handle so that it is easier to see what small changes are going to do with our information and also a visualization of our model results.
5. Automated ensemble model to make it easier to identify some of the performers who are doing the best.
6. A platform that is integrated to handle some of the automation that we need in our data, speeding up the process that we need for the data to decision selection.
7. A model deployment system that is easy so that we are able to get results quickly that are reliable and repeatable.

As we can see here, the algorithms that we want to rely on, along with the right tools are going to be critical when it is time to work on our data analysis process. Having these together and making sure that they are compatible and the right ones for your needs can make a big difference in whether you are going to get the right results with the data that you do collect.

How Does This Fit In with Data Analysis?

Now that we have spent some time taking a look at machine learning and some of the different parts that come with machine learning, it is time to move on to another topic here and shift our focus. We want to take a look at how this machine learning topic is able to fit in with what we are doing with data analysis.

Basically, the data analysis is not going to be complete without the help of machine learning. Machine learning is going to be responsible for creating and handling all of the models and algorithms that we want to work with while analyzing our data. We can't go through and manually do the analyzing of all that data, no matter how much we may like or want to do so. It would take too long and you would never be able to work with the data that you have collected. This is why we need to work with our own model and algorithm to do the searching of the data for us.

This is where machine learning is going to come in. When we can combine machine learning together with the Python language, we are going to open up the door to a ton of different algorithms and models that are just waiting for us to use them when we are ready. These are there to help us sort through any of the data that we would like, and gain a better understanding of what is found inside.

To keep it simple, machine learning is going to provide us with the tools and algorithms that we need in order to put the data through and see what kinds of patterns and relationships are found inside. If we were not able to create those algorithms, then sorting through and understanding that data would seem almost impossible.

As we can see, there are a lot of things that we are able to do when it comes to machine learning. It is often seen as one of the more exciting parts of data analysis because when we are creating the right machine learning model, it means that we are getting to the exciting part of actually sorting through and reading through the data we have, and finding those insights and predictions that are going to bring our business the success that we would like. It may take some time, and it is possible that we will have to go through and try out a few different algorithms along the way. but with the help of machine learning and the algorithms and models that you are able to create with the help of Python, you will get those insights and can put them to good use for your business.

Chapter 9: The Importance of Predictive Analysis and How It Uses Our Data Analysis to Help

The final topic that we need to take a look at here is the importance of predictive analysis, and how we are able to use this to help out with our data analysis and decision-making process within our business. Many times, the data analysis that we have been talking about in this guidebook is going to be used in order to help us make some big decisions throughout the company. We will decide what markets to get into, how to beat out the competition, how to serve the customer better, and even what products we are willing to sell to our customers, all with the help of data analysis.

The predictive analysis is going to be a big part of this process as well. It is the part where we really look to the data that we have collected over all of that time and use it to help us predict what is going to happen in the future. Maybe we will use it to help figure out how the economy is going to behave in five years or to figure out how our winter season will do compared to other similar winter seasons in the past. This is a great way to ensure that a business is able to plan ahead and maximize their profits while minimizing the losses that they will encounter.

To help us start, predictive analysis is going to be the use of a statistical algorithm, data, and machine learning techniques in order to identify the likelihood of future outcomes that are based on the historical data that we are using. The goal with this one is to go beyond knowing what has happened to provide us with the best assessment of what is going to happen in the future.

Though this is something that has been around or a long time, it is finally something that more businesses are focusing their time and attention on. More and more companies are turning to use one of this predictive analysis to help them to increase their own bottom line and ensure that they are going to have a competitive advantage. But why is this process growing so much now, compared to in the past? There are a number of reasons for this including:

1. Computers are cheaper and faster than ever before.
2. A growing amount and type of data, and more interest in using this kind of data to figure out some of the most valuable insights for a customer.
3. Software that is easier to use.
4. Tougher conditions in the economy and a need for a company to differentiate itself from others.

With the help of software that is interactive and easy to use becoming prevalent each day, predictive analytics is no longer going to be kept just n the domain of statisticians any longer. Business analysts and other experts are able to use this kind of technology as well.

Why Is This Analysis So Important

Organizations are turning to work with a predictive analysis more than ever before it is going to help them to handle some of their big problems while uncovering some new opportunities at the same time. there are a lot of ways that we are able to work with data analytics including:

Helping companies to detect fraud. Combining more than one type of analytic method can help to improve the pattern detection and can prevent some of the criminal behavior that we are going to see. As we see cybersecurity turn into a growing concern, a lot of the analytics that is seen with predictive and data analysis are going to be needed. These can help us to examine all of the different actions that happen on a network in real-time to help spot any abnormalities that include zero-day vulnerabilities, fraud, and some advanced persistent threats that may come around.

Another option that companies are able to work with here is optimizing our marketing campaign. Predictive analytics is going to be used to help determine the response that you will get from your customers or the things they choose to purchase. It is also a method that helps companies to work with cross-selling opportunities. Predictive models are going to help businesses not only attract new customers, but also retain and grow some of the most profitable customers to the company.

Predictive analysis is able to help improve operations. Many companies are going to use predictive models to help forecast inventory and manage resources. Airlines are able to use predictive analytics to set ticket prices. Hotels are going to use this to predict the number of guests for any given night to help maximize the occupancy that they are able to get and increase their revenue. Predictive analytics enables an organization to function in a more efficient manner.

The biggest reason that companies are going to work the predictive analysis is that it helps them to reduce the amount of risk that they are dealing with. Credit scores, for example, are going to be used in order to assess the likelihood of default for purchases is a good way to look at the predictive analytics. A credit score is going to be a number that is generated through a predictive model that incorporates all of the relevant data to the creditworthiness of another person.

All companies are going to be able to look through this productive analysis in order to help them to reduce the amount of risk that they want to handle at some point. Other risk-related uses include insurance collections and claims from the customer.

How Predictive Analysis Works

Predictive analysis is going to use some of the known results that we have in order to develop or train a model that is able to be used to help us predict values for different or new data. Modeling is going to provide us with results that are in the form of a prediction. This prediction is going to represent a probability of the target variables, which could be something like revenue, based on the estimated significance from a set of input variables.

This is going to be a bit different than what we are going to see when we talk about descriptive models that are going to help you to understand what happened or a diagnostic model that is meant to help you to understand some of the key relationships that are going on, and then make some determinations of something that has happened. Entire books are going to be devoted to learning analytical methods and techniques. Complete curriculums are going to delve deeply into this subject, but we are going to spend some time checking out the basics and more.

There are going to be two types of models that we are able to work with that are known as predictive. These are going to include classification models and regression models. Both of these are going to be important and will work for a lot of the predictive models that we would like to work with.

To start with, we can work with a classification model that is going to be used to help us predict class membership. For instance, you try to classify whether someone is likely to leave, whether that customer is going to work with a solicitation that you send out, whether a customer is going to be a good or bad credit risk to work with. Usually, the model is going to give us some results that are in the form of 1 or 0 based on the predictions that are being sent to you. 1 is going to be indicative of the event that we are trying to target.

Then we can work with the regression model. This is going to help us to predict a number. There are a lot of different numbers that it is able to predict for you based on what kind of information you are trying to put into the algorithm. For example, we could take a look at how much revenue a customer is going to generate over the next year, or the number of months that we are going to have until a component on one of our machines is going to last.

There are a number of modeling techniques that you are able to work with when it is time to work with this kind of prediction process. The three most common types are going to be neural networks, decision trees, and regression. Let's take a look at how each of these is going to work and why each one is important to the process that we are working with.

To start, we can look at the decision trees. These are a type of classification model that is going to partition the data we have into subsets based on the categories that we have with our input variables. This helps you to understand the path of decision that someone is likely to have. A decision tree is going to look just like a tree that is going to have each branch of it representing a choice between a number of alternatives and each leaf is going to represent a decision or a classification.

The model that we have here is going to take a look at the data and then tries to find the one variable that is able to split up the data into logical groups that are the most different. As a programmer, you will find that these decision trees are going to be popular because they are easy to understand and to interpret when it is time. These decision trees are going to be able to handle some of the missing values that we need and can be used when it is time to select out the variables that we want to work with. So, if you are trying to get an answer that is interpretable without a lot of work, or you want to work with a database that has a lot of missing values, then starting out with a decision tree is a great option to start with.

The second thing that we are going to spend some time working with is a regression. This is a good method to work within statistics and will help us to estimate the relationships that are found in the variables intended for data that is assumed to follow a normal distribution, it is going to work to help us find some key patterns in a large set of data. It can even help us to figure out some of the specific factors that we would like, such as the price.

With this kind of analysis, we are going to work on predicting a number, called the response or a Y variable. With the linear regression, in particular, there is going to be just one variable that is independent that is able to explain and predict the outcome that we will have with Y. But then with multiple regression, we are going to find that we need to rely on more than one variable to help us predict the outcome in the end.

And the other method that we are going to work with is the neural network. These are going to be some of the most sophisticated techniques that we are able to use with machine learning because they have the ability to handle some really complex relationships that are going to show up in your data. They are going to be so popular with data scientists because they are powerful and have a lot of flexibility. The power is going to come with the ability that these neural networks have in handling all of the nonlinear relationships in the data, which is going to become more common as we collect some more data.

There are a lot of times where we are able to work with the neural network, but they are often used to help us confirm some of the findings that we did with the other two methods. Neural networks are going to be based on pattern recognition and some of the processes of artificial intelligence that will graphically model parameters. They are going to work well if you would like to get a prediction, but you do not have a mathematical formula to help you get started.

Other Methods to Use

The three methods that we spent some time talking about, it is time for us to explore a bit more about the other techniques that are present when it comes to working with data analysis and even with predictive analysis. Any of the algorithms that you can work with when it is time to do machine learning will make a big difference as well. Some of the other techniques that you are able to work with include:

1. Bayesian analysis: This is going to be a method that is able to treat the parameters as random variables and then will define probability more as the degrees of belief. When you go through this kind of analysis, you are going, to begin with, the prior belief that you have regarding the probability distribution of an unknown parameter. After learning a lot of information about the data you have, you will then go through and change as well as update your belief about that parameter.

2. Memory-based reasoning: This is going to be a technique that works with the K-Nearest Neighbor algorithm and it is used to help out

with categorizing or predicting the observations that you would like.

3. Partial least squares: This is going to be a flexible statistical technique that we are able to apply to the data of any shape. It is able to model the relationships that happen between the input and the output, even when there is a lot of noise, a lot of different outputs, or there are more inputs than observed. The method of partial least squares is going to look for the factors that are present that can help to explain both the response and predictor variations.

4. Principal component analysis: The purpose of this analysis is to help the analyst to derive a small number of independent linear combinations of a set of variables. These variables need to retain as much as they can of the original variables.

5. Support vector machine: This is going to be a technique of machine learning that is going to use associated learning algorithms in order to help us get through the data and recognize the patterns that are inside. It can be used to help out with both regression and classification.

6. Gradient boosting: This is going to be an approach that is able to take our set of data and resample it several times to generate the results that form a good weighted average. Just like what we see with a decision tree, the boosting is not going to make any assumptions about the distribution of the data.

   a. Boosting is not going to be as prone to overfitting the data like a single data tree, which makes it easier to get the solution that you would like.

7. Ensemble models: This is going to be a model that is able to be produced by training several of the similar models and then combining their results to get the accuracy that you would like, reduce the bias that shows up, reduce variance, and then identify the best model to use with the new data as well.

8. Incremental response: This can also be known as the uplift or the net lift models. These are the models that are going to be used in order to help change up the probability caused by an action. they are going to be used widely in order to reduce the amount of churn that is present and to discover the effects of the different types

of programs that you would like to use with marketing.

9. K-Nearest Neighbor or KNN: This is going to be a non-parametric method for regression and classification that is going to predict the object of a value or class memberships based on the k-closest training examples.

10.   Time series data mining: This kind of time series data is going to be time-stamped and then collected overtime at intervals that you set up. This could be the number of website visits each outer, the calls per day, or the sales that your company makes each month. This kind of mining is going to be able to help us combine some data mining techniques including decision trees, sampling, and clustering are all going to be applied to the data that we can collect over time. the goal with this one is to help improve the predictions that we see.

Working with predictive analysis is going to be one of the best things that you are able to do when it is time to work with some of the processes as well. This is an extension of the process that we are talking about when we look at data analysis. It is able to take some of the work that we did with data analysis, and use it in order to make sure that we can make some smart predictions in this process.

All businesses want to make sure that they are reducing the amount of risk that they are taking on. And these same businesses want to make sure that they are able to make predictions that help them to navigate the right processes to help them succeed, meat the needs of their customers, and to beat out the competition as well.

The predictive analysis is going to help us to get more done in the process. You will find that it helps us to see the different scenarios that are present in the future and see the likely outcome that is going to show up. Then the company or those who are going to make decisions can look at these outcomes and figure out what path they would like to take into the future to help them succeed as well.

Working with predictive analysis is going to be one of the best things that you are able to add to some of the work that we do with machine learning, data analysis, and Python learning. Learning how to work with this process, and more, you will be able to go through and actually make some of the predictions that are needed in order to handle the direction of your business in the future.

Conclusion

Thank you for making it through to the end of *Python Data Analysis*, let's hope it was informative and able to provide you with all of the tools you need to achieve your goals whatever they may be.

The next step is to take some time to learn more about data analysis, and then decide if it is the right process for your business. So many companies, that span a lot of different industries, are able to benefit when they work with data analysis. This allows them to get a lot of the power and control that they want for their respective industries and will ensure that they will be able to really impress their customers and get some good results in the process. Learning how to use a data analysis is going to change the game in how you do business, as long as it is used in the proper manner.

This guidebook has taken some time to explore what data analysis is all about, and how we are able to use this for our benefits as well. There are a lot of business tools out there, but data analysis is designed to help us focus on finding the hidden patterns and insights that are in our data, making it easier to base our decisions on data, rather than intuition and guessing as we did in the past. And when it comes to making sure that we complete the data analysis in the right manner, nothing is better than working with the Python coding language to get things done.

In this guidebook, we spent our time taking a look at data analysis and some of the different parts that come with it. We learned how this process works, and how we are able to combine it together with the Python coding language in order to create strong and efficient, and often fast, algorithms to handle the work that we need. We also took a look at the benefits of the Python language on our data analysis, how to work with the Pandas library to handle some of the algorithms and different parts of data science, and how these two parts are able to come together to give you the results that you want.

At the end of this guidebook, we also took a look at a few of the other topics that are going to be important when you are working on your Python data analysis. We looked at some of the basics that come with machine learning and how this combines together with Python in order to actually create some of the algorithms that you need in data analysis. And then we finished off with a look at predictive analytics and how this can benefit from a strong data analysis to help us learn more about our company and our industry and make the right predictions and decisions to move us to the future.

There are so many aspects that need to come into play when we are working with our own data analysis, and it is important that we take the time to learn how these works, and how to put it all together. And that is exactly what we will do in this guidebook. When you are ready to learn more about Python data analysis, and all of the different parts that come together to help us with understanding our data and how to run our business, make sure to check out this guidebook to help you get started.

Finally, if you found this book useful in any way, a review on Amazon is always appreciated!